Buses, Trams, Trolleybuses Recollections 1962

Henry Conn

Contents

First published in 2017

British Library Cataloguing in Publication Data

A catalogue record for this book is available from the British Library.

Acknowledgements

All the illustrations in this book are from the camera of Tony Belton, and without these wonderful views this book would not have been possible. Tony also prepared much of the text for the London views. My most sincere thanks to Tony – outstanding.

The PSV Circle Fleet Histories for the operators in this book and a number of issues of *Buses Illustrated* were vital sources of information.

Frontispiece: **GLASGOW** On Dumbarton Road working route 26 on 2 June 1962 are Nos 1359 (left) and 1315, Cunarders built by GCT in 1950 and 1949 respectively. Under the bridge is an Alexander-bodied AEC Regent V from the batch of 89 that were delivered between November 1960 and March 1962.

ISBN 978 1 85794 493 8

Silver Link Publishing Ltd
The Trundle
Ringstead Road
Great Addington
Kettering
Northants NN14 4BW

Tel/Fax: 01536 330588
email: sales@nostalgiacollection.com
Website: www.nostalgiacollection.com

Printed and bound in the Czech Republic

Introduction

The first James Bond film, *Dr No*, had its world premiere at the London Pavilion in Piccadilly Circus, a glamorous event launching an obsession that is still with us. The following day *Love Me Do*, the Beatles' first single, was released rather more quietly. It became a Top 20 hit, reaching No 17, largely because the group's manager Brian Epstein, bought 10,000 copies, most of which remained unsold. Prompted by hundreds of requests from Liverpool, *Love Me Do* got its first airing on Radio Luxembourg.

Ian Fleming knew that the Bond films would make him a far richer and more famous man, but he was exhausted and ill, already suffering from the ailments that killed him less than two years later, at the age of 56. Ten days later, and just a couple of hundred miles from where Ursula Andress had emerged bikini-clad from the sea, another plot started to unfold. A US Air Force U-2 plane on a photo-reconnaissance mission spotted a Soviet missile base being constructed in Cuba. For the following fortnight, Russia and America faced each other down – it was the most dangerous moment in human history thus far. Experts at the time calculated that, had the worst attack and retaliation taken place, 215 million people would have died at once. Thankfully, Kennedy did not panic.

The arrival of Bond and the Beatles seems now to have coincided with many other things that signalled the start of a different Britain. In 1962 *That Was The Week That Was* came on television, satirising our leaders for the amusement of the citizenry. Meanwhile John Stephen had four boutiques on Carnaby Street, signalling the start of young men's escape from Burton the Tailor. The Rolling Stones, the Beatles' naughtier cousins, played their first gig at the Marquee Club in Soho. More significantly, the Lord Privy Seal, Edward Heath, spent the year trying to negotiate Britain's tortuous way into the Common

Market. Far more life-changing than any of these, the previous December the Minister of Health, Enoch Powell, announced that the oral contraceptive pill could be prescribed on the NHS at the subsidised price of 2 shillings a month.

1962 was the year that *Z Cars*, with Liverpool and police cars and its harder realism, took over from *Dixon of Dock Green*. The first newspaper colour supplement was launched in February. On 19 May Marilyn Monroe sang *Happy Birthday* to President Kennedy at his Madison Square Garden party, with special lyrics and wearing that special dress. It was Kennedy's 45th birthday. He didn't see 47. Marilyn Monroe was 36, the ultimate goddess of old-fashioned Hollywood sex appeal. We have not seen her like again, nor could we ever. She died less than two months later, failing to survive 1962.

But the Beatles did, and so did James Bond!

Enjoy the nostalgia!

GLASGOW One of the best-known landmarks in Glasgow is the 'Hielanman's Umbrella' in Argyle Street, a tunnel formed by the platforms of Central station above. It was said that Highland visitors and exiles could shelter here for nothing. Working route 9 on 5 June is Coronation No 1265, which was built by Glasgow Corporation Transport (GCT) in 1939.

On this day the Scottish Opera Company is founded by Alexander Gibson.

GLASGOW On route 26 on 1 June is No 1321, a GCT-built Cunarder new in 1950. Beside it, and heading for Castlemilk, is No L52 (FYS 880), an Alexander-bodied Leyland PD2/24 new in September 1957; it became a driver trainer vehicle in July 1970 and passed to the Greater Glasgow Passenger Transport Executive in that role on 1 June 1973.

On this day, Adolf Eichmann, the German SS officer and war criminal, was executed at Ramlah in Israel.

GLASGOW At Bridgeton Cross on 2 June, working service 26, is Coronation No 1284, which had been built by GCT in 1940; note the overhead trolleybus wires.

On this day the last tram car to run to and from Dalmarnock on route 26 was No 1318, departing from the terminus at 12.06am. Car No 1270 was the last car to enter Partick depot, and the depot itself was closed the following day with its surviving trams transferred to Dalmarnock depot.

GLASGOW Under policeman traffic control, here is another busy scene at Bridgeton Cross. Working service 9 is Coronation No 1319, built by GCT in 1950. The lorry on the left belongs to R. Sankey & Son Ltd, Bulwell Potteries. This Nottingham-based company, founded in 1855 by Richard Sankey, was perhaps the best-known manufacturer of earthenware flowerpots in the world. It made use of local raw materials to produce up to 60,000 high-quality clay pots and saucers a day, until 1939 all made by hand. The range was vast, including pots weighing as much as 84lb, and they were all stamped 'Sankey Bulwell'.

Above: **GLASGOW** At Bridgeton Cross on the same day working service 26 is No 1308, a Cunarder new in 1949.

Above: **GLASGOW** This wonderful view shows No LA13 (SGD 591), having broken down, being pushed aside by the public so that the Coronation tram behind can continue its journey. This bus was one of the first Alexander-bodied Leyland PDR1/1s to enter service, in September 1962.

The lorry on the left belongs to J & H Transport Services. A chance meeting between two young men in 1949, Mr F. A. Jeune and Mr W. A. Heymann, led to the foundation of the company, with headquarters in a back street in Peckham where the garage became a transit depot for lorries plying long-distance routes between London and Glasgow, Birmingham and Manchester. Within a year the firm's turnover had reached five figures. During 1954-55 the firm purchased 48 lorries from British Road Services and from there the fleet was modernised until, when this view was taken, it had more than 150 modern vehicles.

Left: **GLASGOW** On a tour of the remaining Glasgow tram system on Argyle Street in late August 1962 is No 1089. This one-off single-deck bogie car was built in 1926 for evaluation on longer-distance inter-urban routes where traffic was being lost to privately operated motor buses. It was later used on the Duntocher service and for shipyard workers' extras, and is now in preservation.

Above: **GLASGOW** The final day of normal public service for trams in Glasgow was 1 September, and this is the scene of an accident at Dalmuir West on that day involving Central SMT No L585 (GM 8825), an Alexander-bodied Leyland PD2/30 new in 1957; the good news is that it was repaired and remained in the fleet until 1972.

Above right: **GLASGOW** The last day of tram operation involved route 9, and passing the accident scene on the same day Coronation car No 1249. In the centre of the view, having repaired damaged overhead wiring, is GYS 351, a Bedford tower wagon.

Right: **GLASGOW** Later on the same day, with No L585 removed from the accident scene, heading for Helensburgh is Central SMT No L601 (GM 9961), an NCME-bodied Leyland PD2/30 new in 1959 and sold for scrap in December 1973.

GLASGOW Following closure there were commemorative services between Anderston Cross and Auchenshuggle, on which special sixpenny tickets were issued. Working on London Road with Celtic Park in the background on Sunday 2 September is No 1240, a Coronation new in 1939.

GLASGOW Also working on that Sunday was Coronation No 1243, also new in 1949. The bus working service 46 to Castlemilk is No L447 (SGD 449), an Alexander-bodied Leyland PD3/2 new in September 1961. At closure there were 62 trams at Dalmarnock depot, and they were all moved under their own power to Coplawhill Works for disposal. The last car to make this journey, on 15 September, was Coronation No 1163. By that date work had already begun to remove the track from Auchenshuggle.

Newcastle-upon-Tyne

Right: **NEWCASTLE-UPON-TYNE** Between March 1948 and November 1950 an ambitious modernisation of the Newcastle Corporation trolleybus fleet was made; a total of 186 new trolleybuses were delivered, comprising 100 three-axle and 86 two-axle types with chassis by BUT and Sunbeam, both intended to replace the original fleet and to expand the system to its maximum extent of 37 route miles covering 28 routes. Reversing at the Wallsend Boundary terminus of route 32 at Fenham on 7 June is No 453 (LBB 53), an MCCW-bodied Sunbeam F4 new in 1949 and sold for scrap in June 1964.

On this day England drew 0-0 with Bulgaria in their 3rd Group game of the World Cup in Brazil.

Left: **NEWCASTLE-UPON-TYNE** Arriving at the route 32 terminus on the same day is No 458 (LBB 58), another MCCW-bodied Sunbeam F4 new in March 1949; it was scrapped in June 1964 in Larkhall.

Right: **NEWCASTLE-UPON-TYNE** The next four photographs were taken on 8 June, by which time six of the MCCW-bodied Sunbeam F4s had been withdrawn from service. Working route 32 to Fenham in the City Centre is No 461 (LBB 61), an MCCW-bodied Sunbeam F4 new in February 1949.

NEWCASTLE-UPON-TYNE At Central Station, about to leave for Gosforth, is No 485 (LTN 485), an MCCW-bodied BUT 9641T that was new in April 1948. It was 8 feet wide and the bodywork was almost identical to that of the London Q1 class (Nos 1765 to 1841), adopted by Newcastle in order to obtain early delivery. Overtaking No 485 on route 42 heading for Heaton Road is No 539 (LTN 539), a Northern Coachbuilders Limited (NCB)-bodied Sunbeam F4 new in January 1950.

NEWCASTLE-UPON-TYNE At its height the city's trolleybus system had 28 routes and a maximum fleet of 204 trolleybuses. Standing at Denton Square terminus is No 498 (LTN 498), another MCCW-bodied BUT 9641T also new in April 1948. In the background, working route 35C, is No 448 (LBB 48), an MCCW-bodied Sunbeam F4 new in January 1949. No 498 would be withdrawn in late 1963, while 498 would be sold for scrap in July 1965.

Right: **NEWCASTLE-UPON-TYNE** Byker Bridge was opened on 18 October 1878 and was originally less than 30 feet wide; it was widened in 1899 to 48 feet. On the bridge working route 35 is No 549 (LTN 549), an NCB-bodied Sunbeam F4 new in March 1950 and sold for scrap in June 1964.

Below: **NEWCASTLE-UPON-TYNE** Moving on to 9 June, when the next eight pictures were taken, departing Grange Estate terminus for Central Station is No 489 (LTN 489), an MCCW-bodied BUT 9641T that was new in March 1948. These trolleybuses spent much of their service lives on the 31, 31A and 31B services.

Below: **NEWCASTLE-UPON-TYNE** No 489 is seen again nearing Central Station; it would be sold for scrap in July 1965.

On this day the No 1 single was Elvis Presley's Good Luck Charm, *while his album* Blue Hawaii *was No 1 in the album charts for 16 weeks.*

NEWCASTLE-UPON-TYNE This view was taken in the early evening of 9 June from the top deck of a BUT trolleybus at the Welbeck Road terminus of route 35C, about to pass No 490 (LTN 490), an MCCW-bodied BUT 9641T new in April 1948.

The previous day Marilyn Monroe had been fired by 20th Century Fox because of her frequent absences from the filming of the movie Something's Got to Give. Over a course of seven weeks of shooting, she had only appeared on five days. Very sadly, less than two months later, on 5 August, she was found dead.

NEWCASTLE-UPON-TYNE Between 1946 and 1951, benefiting from the continuing post-war demand for new bodies or complete vehicles, Northern Coachbuilders Limited constructed a considerable number of bodies for two- and three-axle trolleybuses at its works at Claremont Road, Spital Tongues, Newcastle-upon-Tyne. Working service 34 after a shower on 9 June is No 516 (LTN 516), an NCB-bodied Sunbeam 7 new in November 1948 and sold for scrap in July 1965.

NEWCASTLE-UPON-TYNE If only today's roads were like this! This excellent view shows three Newcastle trolleybuses and a United Bristol bus, and not a lorry in sight. It was taken from another BUT trolleybus, and approaching on route 34 is No 521, an NCB-bodied Sunbeam S7 new in November 1948.

NEWCASTLE-UPON-TYNE The Corporation's last trolleybuses, Nos 579 to 628 (NBB 579 to 628), MCCW-bodied BUT 9641Ts, began to be delivered during May 1950, with the last, Nos 624 to 628, arriving during November 1950. Representing this batch is No 580 (NBB 580), working on route 34A. The passing fire engine is a Commer QX; these were introduced at the 1948 Commercial Motor Show.

1962
No 1 Records (1)

January
Cliff Richard & The Shadows *The Young Ones*

February
Elvis Presley *Rock-A-Hula-Baby / Can't Help Falling In Love*

March
The Shadows *Wonderful Land*

May
B. Bumble & The Stingers *Nut Rocker*
Elvis Presley *Good Luck Charm*

June
Mike Sarne (featuring Wendy Richard) *Come Outside*

July
Ray Charles *I Can't Stop Loving You*
Frank Ifield *I Remember You*

September
Elvis Presley *She's Not You*

October
Tornados *Telstar*

November
Frank Ifield *Lovesick Blues*

December
Elvis Presley *Return To Sender*

NEWCASTLE-UPON-TYNE On service 34 to Wallsend is No 586 (NBB 586), one of the MCCW-bodied BUT 9641Ts, new in June 1950; it would last until the end of the system, being sold for scrap in February 1967. As mentioned earlier, the Newcastle BUTs were essentially the same as London Transport's Class Q1, but did have some interior differences such as the seat covers and polished wooden fittings.

Left: **NEWCASTLE-UPON-TYNE** Working route 42 in Benton Bank, Jesmond Vale, is No 572 (LTN 572), an NCB-bodied BUT 9611T new in March 1949 and sold for scrap in June 1964. On the right is the Flora Robson Playhouse, named in honour of the famous South Shields-born actress; it was demolished in 1971.

Right: **NEWCASTLE-UPON-TYNE** At Welbeck Road terminus on 10 June is No 599 (NBB 599), an MCCW-bodied BUT 9641T new in August 1950.

On this day it was approved unanimously by the Presidium of the Soviet Union to place Soviet nuclear missiles in Cuba. Under the plan, 24 medium-range nuclear missiles and 16 intermediate-range missiles would be placed on the island, and a total of 50,874 Soviet military personnel would be placed there to defend against an invasion.

South Shields, Hull and Doncaster

SOUTH SHIELDS At its maximum, the town's trolleybus system had 11 routes and 61 trolleybuses. Arriving at Pier Head terminus on 10 June is No 200 (CU 3589). This was one of a batch of four Weymann-bodied Karrier E4s, Nos 200 to 203, which were the first new trolleybuses for the South Shields system, which had been inaugurated on 12 October 1936. No 200's chassis was scrapped in 1952 and the body fitted to the chassis of No 205 in 1953, which become the new No 200; it was scrapped in November 1962.

SOUTH SHIELDS In July 1958 South Shields acquired from St Helens eight East Lancashire-bodied Sunbeam F4s, BDJ 74 to 81, which had been new between December 1950 and February 1951. They entered service over a period of a year, and this is No 201 (BDJ 74) Pier Head terminus on the same day. All eight had been withdrawn by April 1963 and the South Shields system closed on 29 April 1964. The clock tower was erected in June 1890 to commemorate Queen Victoria's Jubilee and as a memorial to the first lifeboat designed and built in South Shields in 1790.

SOUTH SHIELDS acquired four Park Royal-bodied Karrier W4s from Pontypridd in April 1957. They were FTG 234, FTG 235, GNY 301 and GNY 302, and all had entered service by September of that year. This is No 238 (FTG 234) on route 4 on 10 June; new in August 1945, it was sold in May 1963.

SOUTH SHIELDS This is No 248 (CU 4718), an NCB-bodied Karrier W4 new in 1947, working route 12 in the early spring of 1962. The first trolleybuses delivered in 1936 were painted royal blue with primrose window frames and waistband, the roofs were mid-grey, and the wheels and mudguards black. The next change came in 1946 when the fleet name South Shields became standard, as seen in this view.

HULL Unless otherwise stated, all the following photographs in and around Hull were taken on 10 July 1962. The city's new trolleybus system was inaugurated on 23 July 1937 with the opening of service 61 to Chanterlands, then two days later service 62 to Newland Avenue began operations. Turning from Princes Avenue into Spring Bank while working service 62 is No 70 (GRH 290), a Brush-bodied Sunbeam W new in June 1945. The railway station on the right is Hull Botanic Gardens, which opened on 8 May 1848 as Hull Cemetery, and was renamed Hull Botanic Gardens on 1 November 1881, staying thus named until closure on 19 October 1964. The station was at street level immediately to the north of a level crossing across Spring Bank, just east of the junction with Princes Avenue. The building was demolished in 1976, and the site is now occupied by a public house.

HULL Seen in Newland Avenue, this is Hull No 78 (GRH 298), a Brush-bodied Sunbeam W new in June 1945; it would be sold for scrap in November 1963.

On this day Telstar 1, the world's first communications satellite, was launched into orbit from Cape Canaveral, and though no longer functional it still orbits the earth. Released on 17 August 1962 was the single Telstar by the Tornados; this instrumental track was named after the satellite and is estimated to have sold at least 5 million copies.

HULL In Holderness Road, with the bridge carrying the former Hull & Barnsley Railway line in the background, is No 96 (HRH 96), a Roe-bodied Sunbeam F4 new in June 1948. Note the Clover milk float; Clover Dairies were based in Grimsby but operated bottling dairies in Hull, Stoke, Middlesbrough and Gloucester. Sterilised milk was processed and bottled in Grimsby and Hull.

Right: **HULL** Corporation acquired 19 Park Royal-bodied AEC Regent IIIs from St Helens Corporation. One of these was No 133 (BDJ 816), which was new in 1952, acquired by Hull in April 1962 and seen here on one of its first days in service; it would eventually be sold for scrap in February 1970. Overtaking it is No 245 (HAT 245), a Weymann-bodied AEC Regent, one of a batch of 16 delivered between August and October 1946. It was withdrawn in August 1966 and passed to Hull City Engineers Department before being sold for preservation in August 1971.

Below: **HULL** Approaching Southcoates level crossing on Holderness Road is No 142 (BDJ 61), another of the former St Helens Weymann-bodied AEC Regent IIIs, this one being new in 1950; it was sold for scrap in June 1971. According to the PSV records, it was acquired in October 1962. yet this view was taken three months earlier.

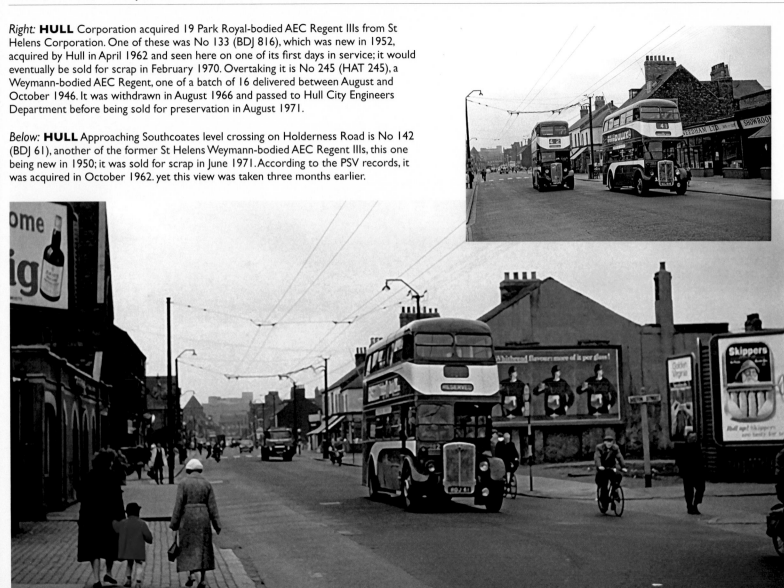

HULL Passing Witham turning circle on service 33 is No 144 (BDJ 66), looking very smart on its first few days in service with Hull Corporation.

The Beatles' first live show in Hull took place at the Majestic Ballroom on 20 October 1962.

Below: **BEVERLEY** One of the town's most famous landmarks is the 15th-century gate known as Beverley Bar, or Beverley North Bar. It is designated a Grade I listed building and is now recorded in the National Heritage List for England, maintained by Historic England. It is located on Lairgate, close to Beverley Minster, and abuts buildings on both sides. Traffic is limited to single file through the bar arch and is controlled by a set of lights. In 1935 the 'Beverley Bar roof' was introduced on East Yorkshire double-deck buses, and this specially shaped roof would appear on most of the company's new double-deck buses until 1970, when road alterations brought an end to the operation of buses under the bar. On 11 July 1962, showing the tight fit for a double-deck bus through the bar, is No 645 (VKH 45), a Willowbrook-bodied AEC Regent V new in November 1956 and scrapped in September 1971.

Above: **HULL** Between April and July 1952 East Yorkshire took delivery of 16 unusual but attractive Roe coach-bodied Leyland PD2/12s, Nos 568 to 583 (MKH 77 to 92). Nos 576 to 583 were downgraded to buses in 1954, but the remainder retained their coach livery, as represented here on Holderness Road on 12 July by No 570 (MKH 79). In the background can be glimpsed the Astoria Cinema, which opened on 30 July 1934 and closed as a cinema on 7 June 1963, to be immediately reopened as the Astoria Bingo Club.

DONCASTER The town's trolleybus system was medium-sized, with six routes – to Bentley (a loop), Beckett Road, Wheatley Road, Racecourse/Hyde Park (loop), Balby and Hexthorpe, all from the city centre – and a maximum fleet of 47 trolleybuses. In early January 1954 Doncaster purchased from Southend Nos 130 to 138 (BHJ 827 to 829 and BHJ 898 to 903), all Sunbeam Ws with bodywork by Park Royal apart from No 130, which had Brush bodywork. All entered service in January 1954, and all received new Roe bodies between 1957 and 1959. In service to Beckett Road on 12 June 1962 is Doncaster No 387 (BHJ 898), which was withdrawn just a short time after this view was taken and the bodywork transferred to Daimler CVG6 No 185.

DONCASTER Following behind No 387, and working the Wheatley road service, is No 388 (BHJ 899), another of the ex-Southend Sunbeam Ws that entered service in January 1954; it received its new Roe body in 1957, and after withdrawal this body was transferred to Daimler CVG6 No 187.

DONCASTER Heading for Beckett Road on the same day is No 354 (FWX 902), a Sunbeam W that was new to Mexborough & Swinton as its No 18 in 1947. It was acquired by Doncaster as a chassis only and was rebodied by Roe in 1957. The last Doncaster trolleybuses ceased operations on 14 December 1963, and No 354 was withdrawn at that time, the body removed and transferred to motorbus No 123 in 1964.

Bradford

BRADFORD All but the last of these Bradford views were taken during a 45-minute period on 6 June 1962. In the first, working route 33 to Eccleshill in Forster Square, is No 626 (AAK 428), which was new in 1935. It originally had English Electric bodywork, but was rebodied by NCB in May 1949. This trolleybus would be sold for scrap later in the year.

On this day Jamaica became independent from the United Kingdom.

Right: **BRADFORD** Working service 25 to Saltaire is No 640 (CAK 640), an AEC 661T new in July 1938 with English Electric bodywork. It received a new Crossley body in March 1952 and remained in the fleet until it was sold for scrap in January 1964.

Far right: **BRADFORD** No 675, another AEC 661T with English Electric bodywork, was new in May 1939. It received a new 8-foot-wide East Lancashire body in May 1956 and re-entered service the following month; it was withdrawn in 1967 and sold for scrap in April 1968.

Right: **BRADFORD**'s No 692 (DKU 692) was new with a Weymann body in January 1940 as a demonstrator. It was purchased by Bradford and was the last Karrier E4 built. In March 1952 it received a new Crossley body and is seen here in Forster Square a short time before it was withdrawn from service. I think the lorry in the right background is an Albion Chieftain.

BRADFORD Because of wartime conditions, an order for 25 8-foot-wide Weymann-bodied Sunbeam MF2s was diverted from Johannesburg Municipal Transport to British operators; ten went to St Helens, five to Nottingham and ten to Bradford. They were allocated fleet numbers 693 to 702 and entered service between June and October 1942. During 1955 all ten of the Bradford examples received new East Lancashire bodywork and re-entered service in January 1956. This is No 701; it was fitted with a sliding door (which can be seen in this view), but this was removed in the latter part of 1962. All ten had been scrapped by September 1967.

The day after this view was taken the Soviet Union conducted the second largest nuclear test in history, exploding a 40-megaton bomb.

Right: **BRADFORD** Between September 1954 and August 1957 Bradford purchased one Karrier E4S and 22 Karrier Ws from Darlington Corporation. However, only nine of them entered service with Bradford, Nos 785 to 793 (GHN 403, GHN 563, GHN 564, GHN 566, GHN 569, GHN 570, GHN 571, GHN 574 and GHN 575), the remainder being stripped of electrical equipment and for spares. All nine received East Lancashire bodywork before entering service. In Forster Square is No 788 (GHN 566), which was acquired in August 1957 and rebodied in December 1958; it was sold for scrap in November 1971.

Far right: **BRADFORD** Passing Forster Square station is No 747 (EKU 747), one of a batch of 12 Roe-bodied BUT 9611Ts that were new between May and December 1949.

The No 1 single at the time was I Remember You by Frank Ifield. (Please do not yodel...)

Right: **BRADFORD** Also passing Forster Square station, at 4.10pm, is No 754 (FKU 754), one of a batch of six Weymann-bodied BUT 9611Ts that new in January 1951. Unfortunately No 754 was involved in an accident in 1963 and never ran again.

At this time the best-selling albums were Pot Luck *by Elvis and the original soundtrack of* West Side Story.

BRADFORD In April 1953 Bradford acquired from Notts & Derby Traction Company 32 trolleybuses; 17 of them were AEC 661Ts dating from 1937 to 1942, the other 15 were BUT 9611Ts that were new in 1949, and all were Weymann-bodied. This is No 765 (NNU 229), one of the BUT 9611Ts of May 1949, which entered service with Bradford in June 1953.

1962 Happenings (1)

January
- BBC screens first episode of the long-running police drama Z Cars
- 93 die in Holland's worst rail disaster, at Harmelen
- Ranger 3 is launched to study the Moon, but misses by 22,000 miles

February
- The Sunday Times becomes the first paper to print a colour supplement
- American pilot Francis Gary Powers is exchanged for captured Soviet spy Rudolf Abel
- Ballet stars Margot Fonteyn and Rudolf Nureyev dance together in London

March
- France and Algeria sign an agreement in Évian-les-Bains ending the Algerian War
- Un Premier Amour, sung by Isabelle Aubret, wins the Eurovision Song Contest

April
- Jawaharlal Nehru is elected Prime Minister of India
- James Hanratty is hanged in Bedford Gaol for the A6 murder
- West Side Story wins Best Picture at the 34th Academy Awards
- The Commonwealth Immigration Bill removes free immigration for the citizens of member states of the Commonwealth
- Ranger 4 spacecraft crashes into the Moon

BRADFORD Between February and June 1958 Bradford Corporation purchased from Birds of Stratford-upon-Avon 25 former London Transport AEC Regent IIIs, and they were allocated fleet numbers 401 to 425. Representing this batch at Forster Square on 6 August 1962 is No 410 (HLW 159), with a Park Royal body. New in September 1947, it would be sold into preservation from November 1968.

The day before, 5 August, Graham Hill won the German Grand Prix at the Nurburgring. and Nelson Mandela was arrested and lost his freedom for 27 years.

Huddersfield

Below: **HUDDERSFIELD** Paddock is a mile south-west of Huddersfield town centre, and seen there on 5 August is No 493 (AVH 493), a Karrier E6 that was new on 10 August 1938 with Park Royal bodywork. Using Roe frames, No 493 was rebodied by the Corporation in August 1950; further work completed by the Corporation at that time included extensive refurbishment of the chassis, control equipment and traction motor. The trolleybus was withdrawn on 31 October 1962.

Above: **HUDDERSFIELD** At the Longwood terminus a platform was built out over a field and supported on stanchions. The platform carried a turntable for a while, but was later used as a reversing point, as seen here on 7 August with No 519 (AVH 519). This Karrier was new on 1 January 1940 with bodywork by Weymann, was rebodied by Roe in November 1953, and was withdrawn at the end of October 1962.

Right: **HUDDERSFIELD** Out of service in Market Street and heading for Longroyd Bridge Depot on the same day is Karrier No 525 (AVH 525), which was also new on 1 January 1940 with Weymann bodywork. It was rebodied by Roe in March 1953, and withdrawn on 30 January 1963.

HUDDERSFIELD Passing 'The Electricians' on that same August day is No 529 (BVH 129), a Karrier new in March 1939 with Park Royal bodywork; it was rebodied by Roe in February 1953 and withdrawn in January 1963. Hammonds Ales first brewed beer in Manchester Road in Bradford, but production there ceased in 1955 with all brewing moving to Huddersfield (Lockwood Brewery, which closed in 1963) and Tadcaster Tower Brewery (also until 1963). Hammonds was acquired by United Breweries in 1960, which merged with Charrington in 1962.

1962 Happenings (2)

May
- Norwich City wins the English League Cup, beating Rochdale in the final
- 160 die in a triple-train disaster near Tokyo
- 12 East Germans escape via a tunnel under the Berlin Wall
- Juan Carlos of Spain marries the Greek Princess Sophia in Athens
- The new Coventry Cathedral is consecrated

June
- Acker Bilk's Stranger On The Shore becomes the first British record to reach No 1 in the US charts
- Frank Morris, John Anglin and Clarence Anglin escape from the Alcatraz Island prison
- BBC's Steptoe and Son makes its debut
- Brazil beats Czechoslovakia 3-1 to win the 1962 World Cup
- An Air France Boeing 707 jet crashes in Guadeloupe, killing all 113 on board. It is the airline's second fatal accident in just three weeks, and the third fatal 707 crash of the year

July
- American artist Andy Warhol premieres his Campbell's Soup Cans exhibit in Los Angeles
- Telstar, the world's first commercial communications satellite, is launched into orbit and later in the month relays the first trans-Atlantic television signal
- The Rolling Stones make their debut at London's Marquee Club

Far left: **HUDDERSFIELD** Turning from Northumberland Street into John William Street on service 41 to Paddock on 5 August is No 542 (CVH 742), an East Lancashire-bodied Karrier (Sunbeam) MS2 new on 1 August 1947, and withdrawn in June 1964. In the background is the Princess Cinema, which was originally built as a wool merchant's warehouse. It was converted to the Princess Picture House, and opened on 19 May 1923, designed by local Huddersfield architect Clifford Hickson; it closed as a cinema on 24 April 1982, showing Richard Gere in *Yanks*.

Left: **HUDDERSFIELD** Passing the 'Bay Horse' in Acre Street, Marsh, is No 559 (DVH 59), which entered service on 2 February 1948; it was rebodied by East Lancashire in April 1956 and sold for scrap on 30 January 1963.

HUDDERSFIELD The depot at Longroyd Bridge, which was formerly used as a tramway generating station, was taken over by the Electrical Department in 1917 and entirely reconstructed in 1937. It was capable of housing all the 116 trolleybuses owned by the Corporation. Leaving the depot working a football special on 5 August is No 590 (ECX 190), a Park Royal-bodied Sunbeam MS2 new on 1 March 1949 and withdrawn in mid-July 1965.

Sadly, this was the day that Marilyn Monroe was found dead at her home.

HUDDERSFIELD Working route 40 on 7 August is No 638 (PVH 938), an East Lancashire-bodied Sunbeam S7A new on 1 December 1959. It was one of a batch of 10 Sunbeam S7A trolleybuses that entered service in Huddersfield in November and December of that year to replace some of the ageing rebuilt Karrier E6 trolleybuses. These were Huddersfield's last new trolleybuses and also the last three-axle trolleybuses built for service in the United Kingdom. They followed the style of the previous Huddersfield vehicles (three-axle 7ft 6in-wide double-deckers) to fit in with the rest of the fleet, despite the regulations having been relaxed a few years earlier, which would have enabled them to be built as two-axle vehicles. They were not particularly well-liked by the Huddersfield crews, who tried to have alternative vehicles allocated to them.

Blackpool and Fleetwood

Above: **BLACKPOOL** On a tour at Marton Depot on 25 October is 'Boat' No 227, which was one of a batch of 10 'luxury toastracks' new between July and August 1934; the windscreen was fitted in 1958.

Right: **BLACKPOOL** Departing from Talbot Road bus station on service 15B on 28 October is No 217 (DFV 117), a Burlingham-bodied Leyland PD2/5 new in October 1949. The Leyland chassis was modified to take the Burlingham bodywork and was a development of the pre-war design; the Blackpool PD2/5 featured air brakes, concealed radiators and the Blackpool 'V' front. No 217 was the first of the batch to be withdrawn, in October 1963, and was scrapped by the Corporation in April of the following year.

On this day, in an agreement worked out by Khrushchev and Kennedy, with the assistance of UN Secretary-General U Thant, the US pledged not to invade Cuba, and to remove missiles that had been placed in Turkey near its border with the USSR.

Right: **FLEETWOOD** Arriving on service 14, also on 28 October, is No 293 (EFV 293), a Burlingham-bodied Leyland PD2/5 new in September 1951. This batch, Nos 255 to 300 (EFV 255 to 300), was similar to Nos 201 to 249 new in 1949. No 293 was scrapped by November 1968.

The No 1 album on this day was The Shadows with Out of the Shadows.

Far right: **BLACKPOOL** Mr Franklin, who replaced Mr Luff as General Manager of the town's Transport Department in 1954, did not favour the centre-entrance double-deck bodywork, and from 1957 through to 1968 Blackpool began an association with Metropolitan-Cammell Carriage Works, which built 45 Leyland PD2s and 90 Leyland PD3s. This view of No 360 (YFR 360), a Leyland PD3/1, was taken on that same October day, by which time it had been in service for less than three months. The 26 was the bus service that replaced the Marton tram service, and the 20 Leyland PD3/1s, new in 1962, were regular performers.

Right: **LITTLE BISPHAM** Having run more or less alongside the sea all the way from Starr Gate, at Little Bispham the tramway turns inland for the remainder of the journey through Cleveleys and Rossall to Fleetwood. There is a single-track turning circle here, and on the circle on 25 October is Twin car No 272 plus trailer; this tram was rebuilt from Series 2 Railcoaches and entered service in September 1960.

Above: **BLACKPOOL** Standing in the town's bus station on 26 October, after completing an X60 express service from Manchester, is Ribble No 1312 (DRN 252), an all-Leyland PD2/3 new in 1950; this bus was the first of the batch of 50 to be withdrawn, in February 1964.

Born on this day in London was Cary Elwes, who I best remember for his role as Robin Hood in Mel Brooks's comedy Men in Tights.

Above right: **FLEETWOOD** At the junction of Preston Street and Lord Street, also on 26 October, is No 2501 (BCK 444), a Leyland PD1A that was new in 1947 and was originally fitted with bodywork by Brush. During 1955 a number of the Brush-bodied PD1As were rebodied with Burlingham low-height 8-foot-wide bodies and fitted with 9.8-litre engines, being thus reclassified as PD1/3s. No 2501 would be withdrawn in January 1966.

Right: **BLACKPOOL** Entering Marton depot on the same day is No 208, a Series 1 Railcoach new in January 1934. This tram had a 'VAMBAC' multi-notch control system made by Allen West on behalf of Crompton Parkinson, fitted in December 1946. No 208 was withdrawn from service two days after this view was taken, at the closure of the Marton route, and was scrapped at Marton depot during March 1963.

BLACKPOLD Turning into Lord Street from Ash Street on 27 October is No 2634 (CCK 622), an all-Leyland PD2/3 new in 1948. It was one of a batch of 30 that was originally intended for Cape Town, South Africa, but diverted to Ribble when that order was cancelled. This bus was transferred to Scout in April 1963 and sold in April 1965.

BLACKPOOL On the Promenade on 25 October is car No 248, originally open-topped in October 1934 but fitted with a top cover in September 1941. It originally had double destination indicators (as seen in the car following), but these were replaced by diamond-shaped panelling incorporating a single indicator.

On the previous day the US Navy blockade against Soviet ships heading for Cuba began at 10.00am (Washington DC time). Some of the Soviet freighters altered their courses to avoid the confrontation, while others proceeded.

1962 Happenings (3)

July (continued)
- Prime Minister Harold Macmillan dismisses a third of his Cabinet

August
- Marilyn Monroe dies from an overdose of sleeping pills
- Nelson Mandela is arrested and charged with incitement to rebellion
- Beatles drummer Pete Best is fired and replaced by Ringo Starr
- A failed assassination attempt is made against French President Charles De Gaulle
- John Lennon secretly marries Cynthia Powell

September
- The first Cortina rolls off Ford's production line at Dagenham
- The Soviet Union agrees to send arms to Cuba
- Glasgow Corporation runs its last trams
- A flash flood in Barcelona kills more than 440 people

October
- Dr No, the first James Bond film, premieres in UK theatres
- The Beatles release their first single for EMI, *Love Me Do*

Above: **BLACKPOOL** The 'Coronations' were the most luxurious cars ever built for Blackpool and were popular with the public. Behind the scenes, however, they had to be re-panelled using lighter aluminium panels, roof windows had to be panelled over and the 'VAMBAC' equipment proved troublesome. The loans and costs of running the trams almost bankrupted the Transport Department. At Ash Street, departing for Fleetwood on 26 October, is 'Coronation' car No 319, new in May 1953 and seen here with its 'VAMBAC' control equipment, with which it was fitted when new; this tram would be the last of the batch of 18 to have this equipment removed, in February 1970, and would be scrapped at Rigby Road yard in September 1976.

Above right: **BLACKPOOL** In 1961 the North Station route was cut back to outside the Odeon Cinema on Dickson Road, and a trolley reverser was fitted at the terminus; that year also saw the end of the Pantograph cars on the North Station route when they were replaced by railcoaches from the Squires Gate route. In October 1963 it was realised that two routes to Fleetwood were not needed, as passenger numbers had fallen, and the North Station route was closed as far as Gynn Square, together with Bispham Depot, leaving the Promenade route on its own. This unidentified car is seen at Gynn Square on 27 October.

Above: **BLACKPOOL** Another unidentified car is seen en route to Talbot Square on the Marton route, also on 27 October, with Blackpool Tower in the background.

On this day, at 11.19am Washington time, USAF Major Anderson became the only combatant fatality of the Cuban Missile Crisis when his U-2 aircraft was shot down by a surface-to-air missile while he was flying over Cuba.

Brown's Blue of Markfield

LEICESTER During September 1947 No RT173 (HLW 160) entered service from Leyton depot with a Park Royal roofbox body. During January 1957 it received Park Royal body No 4767 during an overhaul in Aldenham, and was then transferred to Plumstead. Withdrawn from service in March 1958, the bus was sold to Birds of Stratford-upon-Avon, which sold it to Brown's Blue Coaches of Markfield the following month. This view was taken in Leicester bus station on 11 January 1962. HLW 160 would pass to Ronsway Coaches Ltd of Hemel Hempstead in March 1963.

On this day the Russian submarine B37 exploded in Polarny naval base due to a fire in the torpedo room; 122 were killed by the explosion, the force of which hurled the submarine's anchor nearly 1.2 miles from the dock.

MARKFIELD On 9 November 1962 the *Coalville Times* announced that Brown's Blue was to be taken over by Midland Red. Negotiations between the company, Midland Red and the Traffic Commissioners continued into the following year, and the last day of operation was 15 March 1963. Midland Red took over the public service routes and the operations at the Markfield (Shaw Lane) depot, and almost all the double-deckers were driven to a parking area next to the Copt Oak public house and made ready for disposal. This is No RT419 (HLX 236), which was new in September 1947 with a Weymann roofbox body and entered service at Leyton depot. Like HLW 160 above, it was stored in March 1958 and sold to Birds in June, being purchased by Brown's Blue that month. It was sold to Smith of Upper Heyford at the end of Brown's Blue operations in March 1963.

Greater London

HAMMERSMITH No 1114 is on route 657 on its way to Hounslow, and is turning right from Goldhawk Road into Chiswick High Road at Youngs Corner. The railway bridge at Stamford Brook Underground station can be seen in the distance, and a beautiful enamel sign pointing the way to it can be seen on the left. The adverts on this particular trolleybus were the nearest we got to all-over adverts at the time, with Associated Redifussion Television having rented all the advertising panels on the vehicle.

Young's Corner is where Chiswick ends and Hammersmith begins. As Chiswick High Road becomes King Street, the shop on the corner of Goldhawk Road was the first in London, for this was the boundary between Middlesex and the old County of London. It was named 'Young's Corner' in 1882 when it became a fare stage for the horse-drawn trams. Demolished when the whole area was developed, it was replaced by the present Victorian redbrick building with a commemorative plaque, 'Rebuilt Youngs Corner 1894', beneath its decorative tower.

CHISWICK It is Bank Holiday Monday, 23 April 1962, and the day of the Aldermaston March. In Chiswick High Road No 1060 (EXV 60), on route 657, has become de-wired at the 'frog' that allowed the trolleybus to turn left into Goldhawk Road at Youngs Corner on its journey to Shepherds Bush. No 1506 (FXH 506), on route 667 to Hammersmith, is slowly edging past No 1060, hoping not to become de-wired itself, which would cause extra problems; once clear, it will go straight ahead, crossing Goldhawk Road into King Street.

The Aldermaston marches were anti-nuclear weapons demonstrations in the 1950s and 1960s and took place on Easter weekend, walking between the Atomic Weapons Research Establishment at Aldermaston in Berkshire and London, a distance of 52 miles. At their height in the early 1960s they attracted tens of thousands of people and were the highlight of the Campaign for Nuclear Disarmament. The first major Aldermaston march took place at Easter 1958, between 4 and 7 April.

ISLEWORTH By coincidence we see No 1060 again on route 657, this time going to Hounslow in London Road, Isleworth, crossing the junction with Twickenham Road at Busch Corner.

CHISWICK It would be impossible to climb on to Chiswick Flyover to take photographs today, but in 1962 it was different, although I have no idea what the reaction of the police would have been if they had seen the photographer! Captured in this view is KI class No 1103 on route 657 on its way to Shepherds Bush. Note the police box and pole-mounted air-raid siren on the right.

1962 Happenings (4)

October (continued)•
- Pictures of Soviet missile silos in Cuba, taken by US spy planes, spark the Cuba Missiles Crisis
- The Fab Four make their TV debut on *People and Places*

November
- The United Nations passes a resolution condemning South Africa's apartheid policies
- In response to the Soviet Union agreeing to remove its missiles from Cuba, US President John F. Kennedy ends the blockade of the Caribbean nation
- Satire show *That Was The Week That Was* is broadcast on the BBC
- An agreement is signed between Britain and France to develop the Concorde supersonic aircraft

December
- David Lean's epic film *Lawrence of Arabia,* starring Peter O'Toole and Omar Sharif, premieres in London
- Britain agrees to purchase Polaris missiles from the US
- The biggest freeze in living memory hits Britain. There are no frost-free nights from 22 December until 5 March 1963

Above: **BRENTFORD** It is Bank Holiday Monday, 23 April 1962, and London Transport has put Extras on route 667 from Hampton Court to Brentford Half Acre; the crowds at Hampton Court on Bank Holidays were such that the normal service couldn't cope. No 1381 is seen here, very smartly turned out bearing in mind it was only 15 days before the demise of the trolleybus in London. It is turning right from St Paul's Road into High Street, departing from Brentford Half Acre on a short working. The crew have kindly altered the front destination from Hampton Court to Brentford Half Acre to facilitate the photograph.

Above right: **ISLEWORTH** No 1276, also on route 657, has completed its spell of duty for the day and is seen turning right into Isleworth depot, on London Road, from the Shepherds Bush direction. When the final trolleybus entered the depot on 8 May 1962 it would be closed, the replacement motorbuses being operated by Hounslow bus garage.

Right: **HOUNSLOW** London K1 class trolleybuses Nos 1058 and 1290, both on route 657, are photographed at Hounslow terminus with No RT1168 (JXC 476) passing on route 117 for Lower Feltham. When this picture was taken, the bus, new in June 1949, was allocated to Hounslow depot, transferring to Uxbridge in May 1962. Although there was only a matter of weeks before the trolleybuses would be withdrawn, they were still kept in very good order by the staff at Isleworth depot.

1962 Arrivals & Departures

ARRIVALS

Jim Carrey	Actor and comedian	17 January
Sam Phillips	Singer	28 January
Axl Rose	Rock musician	6 February
Garth Brooks	Country singer	7 February
Sheryl Crow	Singer	11 February
Lou Diamond Phillips	Actor	17 February
Vanessa Feltz	TV presenter	21 February
Jon Bon Jovi	Rock musician	2 March
Sir Steve Redgrave	Rower	23 March
MC Hammer	Rap singer	30 March
Philip Schofield	TV presenter	1 April
Vincent Gallo	Actor	11 April
Jimmy White	Snooker player	2 May
Danny Huston	Film director	14 May
Paula Abdul	Singer and dancer	19 June
Amanda Donohoe	Actress	29 June
Tom Cruise	Actor	3 July
Neil Morrissey	Actor	4 July
Pam Shriver	Tennis player	4 July
Wesley Snipes	Actor	31 July
Ruud Gullit	Footballer	1 September
Jack Dee	Comedian	24 September
Ally McCoist	Footballer	24 September
Evander Holyfield	Boxer	19 October
Nick Hancock	Actor and TV presenter	25 October
Sharron Davies	Swimmer	1 November
Demi Moore	Actress	11 November
Jodie Foster	Actress	19 November
Ralph Fiennes	Actor	22 December

DEPARTURES

'Lucky' Luciano	American gangster (b1897)	26 January
Eduard von Steiger	President of Switzerland (b1881)	10 February
Halliwell Hobbes	English actor (b1877)	20 February
Arthur Compton	Physicist (b1892)	15 March
Stuart Sutcliffe	Ex-Beatle (b1940)	10 April
Sir Frederick Handley Page	Aircraft manufacturer (b1885)	21 April
Vita Sackville-West	Landscape gardener (b1892)	2 June
William Faulkner	Writer (b1897)	6 July
Marilyn Monroe	Actress (b1926)	5 August
Graham Walker	Motorcycle racer (b1896)	7 September
Eleanor Roosevelt	US First Lady (b1884)	7 November
Queen Wilhelmina	Netherlands (b1880)	28 November
Charles Laughton	Actor and director (b1899)	15 December

Above: **TWICKENHAM** It is nearly 3 o'clock and people are eagerly waiting for the arrival of Diddler No 1 and No 1521 on their special farewell afternoon trip on 8 May 1962. This view, taken in King Street, shows No 1407 (FXH 407) on route 601 turning at Twickenham terminus ready for its return journey to Tolworth.

Above right: **TWICKENHAM** During June 1957 London Transport received from ECW No CRL4 (Coach Routemaster Leyland 4). It was sent to Romford for driver training, then to Chiswick the following month for modifications. From October 1957 it began operations on the 721 route from Romford, and from January 1958 service 711 from Reigate. From July 1958 it worked the 704 from Windsor, and two months later worked the 715 from Hertford. From July 1959 No CRL4 was in service on the 718 from Windsor, and in August 1960 was working the 716 from Stevenage. Around this time the bus received a repaint into a light green livery, and continued to work on the 716 from Stevenage until August 1961, when it was renumbered RMC4. This view of the bus, SLT 59, was taken on 1 May at the Twickenham trolleybus route 601 turning circle. In November 1962 it was repainted to Lincoln Green.

Right: **KINGSTON** Chassisless trolleybus L3 class No 1380 (FXF 380) is photographed on route 604 on its journey to Hampton Court. The vehicle is in Clarence Street in Kingston, passing the junction with Eden Street. At that time it could not have been imagined that such a large establishment as C&A, which can be seen clearly in the background, would close. The FXF registration on No 1380 was unique, being the only one in the fleet; No 1379 was EXV and No 1381 was FXH.

Photo	DESTINATIONS
87	KINGSTON
88	KINGSTON
89	KINGSTON
90	KINGSTON
91	SURBITON
92	HAMPTON
93	HAMPTON
94	HAMPTON
95	HAMPTON
96	HAMPTON
97	HAMPTON
98	RAYNES PARK

Right: **KINGSTON** It is just coming up to a quarter to four in the afternoon and the peak hour is about to begin. This view of No 1390 (FXH 390) on route 602 to The Dittons via Surbiton was taken outside Kingston bus station in Clarence Road. The railway bridge at Kingston station is visible in the distance.

Below left: **KINGSTON** No 1401 (FXH 401) on route 603 to Tolworth Red Lion is passing LT tower wagon TXV 909, which was housed next to 141 London Road, Kingston. In the background can be seen the very impressive Norbiton church. After the closure of the London trolleybus system on 8 May 1962 the tower wagon was sold to Reading Corporation Transport for further service.

Below right: **KINGSTON** Route 605 was extended from Teddington to Twickenham on Sundays, and working the route here is No 1411 (FXH 411), crossing Kingston Bridge at Horse Fair and approaching the roundabout at the junction with High Street Hampton and Hampton Court Road. The destination blind shows Twickenham via Teddington.

Above left: **KINGSTON** No 1528 (FXH 528), one of five Class L3 trolleybuses with sliding rather than drop windows, is on a Kingston short working. Parked in St James's Road, on the Kingston one-way system, it will wait for the scheduled time to depart to either Wimbledon or Hampton Court. Overtaking is green Country No RT3046 (KXW 155) on route 406, which terminated at Kingston.

Left: **SURBITON** No 1381 (FXH 381) is viewed opposite the Ritz Cinema in St Mark's Hill, Surbiton. Working route 601 to Twickenham, it is approaching Surbiton station, where it will turn right into Claremont Road.

Above: **HAMPTON** On Hampton Court Road, between Church Street at Hampton and just before the terminus at Hampton Court, the trolleybuses on route 667 ran alongside the River Thames. Here we see No 1386 en route to Hampton Court; although this was a fast stretch of road, disappointingly the trolleybuses would sometimes crawl along if they were 'running early'.

Above left: **HAMPTON** Route 725 was the first orbital Green Line route, providing a service around the south of London. Introduced in July 1953 and operated by RFs between Windsor and Gravesend, the route was immediately successful and was soon doubled in frequency as far as Dartford. It was worked from Northfleet (NF), Dartford (DT, from 1954), Staines (ST) and Windsor (WR) garages. This is No RF137 (MLL 524), an AEC Regal IV, at Hampton Court running alongside the River Thames on 1 May. No RF137 was based at Northfleet depot from July 1960 until October 1964, when it was sold to G.W. Osborne & Sons of Tollesbury; it remained there until July 1970, when it was sold for scrap.

Left: **HAMPTON** Working another Sunday route 605, this time in the opposite direction, No 1433 (FXH 433) is en route to Wimbledon via Teddington passing under the railway bridge at Hampton Wick station. It is entering High Street, Hampton, from Upper Teddington Road.

Above: **HAMPTON** No 1473 (FXH 473) on route 667 is actually on its way to Hampton Court; the destination blind is showing Hammersmith, having been turned prematurely for its return journey. The trolleybus is in Church Street, Hampton, and is waiting to turn left into Hampton Court Road.

Left: **HAMPTON** No 1495 (FXH 495) is photographed in Hampton Road passing the Watneys public house 'The Jolly Blacksmith' on the corner of South Road. The vehicle is en route to Hampton Court and will cross into Wellington Road to pass Fulwell depot.

Below left: **HAMPTON** Bank Holiday Mondays saw bus routes 14 and 27 extended to Hampton Court; route 14 would come all the way from Hornsey Rise and route 27 from Highgate Archway station. Tony Belton lived at Upper Holloway so he would get the 14 to Hampton Court in the morning and return on the 27 in the evening. This view taken, on 23 April 1962, shows No RTW48 (KGK 548) on route 14 overtaking trolleybus No 1518 (FXH 518) on route 604 at Hampton Court terminus, with an RTL on route 27 in the background. When this view was taken, No RTW48 was allocated to Putney depot, and from late 1963 became a driver trainer until August 1970, when it was sold into preservation.

Below: **RAYNES PARK** No 1516 (FXH 516) is on the Monday-to-Saturday route 605 from Teddington to Wimbledon; as mentioned previously it was extended from Teddington to Twickenham on Sundays. The trolleybus is passing the magnificent 'Carters Tested Seeds Ltd' building at Raynes Park. In 1967 the land was sold, the building demolished, and the land developed by Merton Council to form the Carters Housing Estate.

Above: **HOUNSLOW** Nearest the camera working route 117 to Lower Feltham, is No RT2048 (LUC 296), an AEC Regent III that was new in January 1951. On the left Nos RT693 (JXC 56) and RT4366 (NLP 531) are both working route 116 to Bedfont Green; the former was new in June 1948 and the latter in August 1953. All three buses were working from Hounslow garage when this view was taken.

Left: **EDGWARE** Working service 240A between Edgware Station and Mill Hill East Station on 3 July is No TD99 (JXC 292), a Mann Egerton-bodied Leyland PS1 that was new in May 1949 and entered service on routes 201 and 216. By June 1959 it was working from Edgware garage on the 240A until its withdrawal on 10 October 1962. This was the last route operated by TDs in London, and RFs took over the route.

Actor Tom Cruise was born in Syracuse, New York, on this day.

Left: **FULWELL** It is 20 July and this is No RT1917 (LLU 837) near Fulwell, having left Aldenham after overhaul and heading for Peckham garage, where it would be stationed until July 1966, eventually being sold for scrap in June 1970.

On this day the world's first regular passenger hovercraft service was introduced, a 20-mile run between Rhyl in Wales and Wallasey.

Middle: **EDGWARE** On 12 July we see No RT1314 (KLB 563), a Saunders roofbox AEC Regent III that entered service from Forest Gate on service 25B in February 1950. During January 1958, during overhaul in Aldenham, it was rebodied with a Weymann roofbox body and was allocated to Holloway garage. In May 1961 it was transferred to Harrow Weald garage, where it was used on the 114. Five months after this view was taken No RT1314 was bought by the United Kingdom Atomic Energy Authority.

The Rolling Stones were on stage for the first time under that name at London's Marquee Club in Oxford Street.

Bottom: **CAMDEN TOWN** On the Greenland Road stand at Camden Town on route 31 is No RTW279 (KXW 379), an all-Leyland PD2/3 new in March 1950 and allocated to Harrow Weald garage for routes 140 and 142. By the time this view was taken on 30 July the bus was allocated to Battersea garage; it would be purchased by Ceylon Transport Board in December 1966.

On this day Marilyn Monroe made a final telephone call to the US Justice Department, six days before her death. She had been a regular caller to US Attorney General Robert F. Kennedy, and historians speculate that he told her during the 8-minute phone call that they could no longer see each other. Monroe's phone records were confiscated by the FBI, but Kennedy's were donated to the National Archives after his death.

Below: **PARK ROYAL** Leaving Park Royal Vehicles' factory in Abbey Road, north-west London, on 30 September is Nottingham's No 47 (47 NAU), a Park Royal-bodied Daimler CRG6LX; unfortunately it would be destroyed by fire in December 1977. On the right, No RM1326 (326 CLT), a Park Royal-bodied AEC Routemaster, would enter service from Mortlake garage in December 1962 and remain there for its entire service life, being withdrawn in November 1982 and sold for scrap a year later.

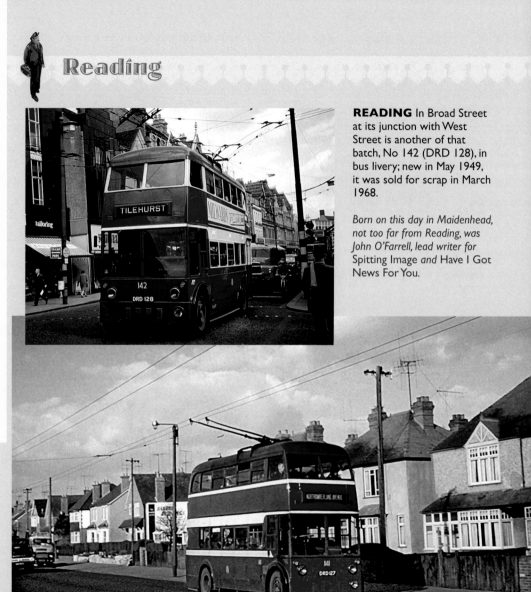

Above: **UPTON PARK** RT114, (FXT 289) began its service life in September 1941, (built and bodied in June 1940), from Putney garage. During May 1955 it was re-painted green and transferred to Hertford garage where it remained until August 1957 when it was withdrawn and stored at Potters Bar garage: RT114 emerged in December 1957 as a trainer and is seen here on 2nd May in this role working from Upton Park. It was sold in May 1963 for scrapping.

READING Twenty Park Royal-bodied BUT 9611Ts were delivered to Reading between March and August 1949; numbered 138 to 157 (DRD 124 to 143), they were the first 8-foot-wide trolleybuses in the fleet and the first with driver-operated platform doors. On Basingstoke Road on 27 March is No 141 (DRD 127), which would be sold for scrap in January 1967.

READING In Broad Street at its junction with West Street is another of that batch, No 142 (DRD 128), in bus livery; new in May 1949, it was sold for scrap in March 1968.

Born on this day in Maidenhead, not too far from Reading, was John O'Farrell, lead writer for Spitting Image and Have I Got News For You.

Left: **READING** Turning from Buckland Road into Basingstoke Road on 18 October is No 153 (DRD 139), another of the Park Royal-bodied BUT 9611Ts, this one new in August 1949 and sold for scrap in January 1967. All 20 were popular trolleybuses and with their purchase electrification of Whitley Estate was completed.

Middle: **READING** Numerically the first of a batch of 12 Park Royal-bodied Sunbeam S7s, this is No 170 (ERD 141) in Caversham Road at its junction with Tudor Road on 27 March. Beneath the bridge is bus No 82 (CRD 871), a Park Royal-bodied AEC Regent II new in November 1948 and sold for scrap in July 1964.

Bottom: **READING** On the reverser at Whitley Wood terminus on the same day is No 176 (ERD 147), another of the S7s, new in December 1950. The Whitley Wood trolleybus route began operation on Sunday 7 August 1949, some two months after the start of the Northumberland Avenue route; trolleybuses used a reverser at the 'Engineers Arms'. During the 1960s there was a plan to link the two routes with new wiring along Whitley Wood Road, but this came to nothing. The Whitley Wood route was the first of the Reading trolleybus routes to cease operating, on Sunday 8 January 1967. Trolleybus No 185 operated the 1.30pm journey from St Mary's Butts to Whitley Wood and the 1.45pm return, becoming the last trolleybus to operate along this road.

Below: **READING** In Broad Street on 21 October is No 185 (VRD 185), a Burlingham-bodied Sunbeam F4A new in July 1961 and one of a batch of 12 that were the last new trolleybuses delivered to Reading. Of this batch, Nos 183 to 186 and 192 would be sold to Teesside Municipal Transport in February 1969 for further service, and all would be sold in April 1971, only No 186 escaping the scrapman to be sold into preservation.

Above right: **READING** To the left of this view is No 179 (ERD 150), an S7 new in December 1950, and it has just suffered a de-wirement. Repairing the damage is No 33 (CDP 583), a Commer Superpoise tower wagon; new in July 1946, it was transferred to the Reading Borough Council street lighting department in February 1969, and sold into preservation in May 1972.

Cardiff

Right: **CARDIFF** Trolleybus operations in Cardiff started on 1 March 1942, St David's Day, with a service between the city centre at Wood Street and the docks at Clarence Road, using five AEC 664T trolleybuses. Delivery of the remaining five trolleybuses of the same model enabled the route to be extended northwards along Cathedral Road to Llandaff Fields. At Roath depot on 15 November, representing the first batch of Cardiff trolleybuses, is No 204 (CKG 194), an NCME-bodied AEC 664T new in 1942; it would be sold for scrap in 1965

Below left: **CARDIFF** Encouraged by the results of the trolleybuses, the Cardiff Transport Department engineer prepared a design for a post-war trolleybus in cooperation with East Lancashire Coachbuilders. Working towards Pengam on 15 November 1962, a route that had been opened on the same day 12 years earlier in 1950, is No 225 (DUH 720), an East Lancashire-bodied BUT 9641T new in 1948 and one of the first 20 based on the wartime design. Cardiff Corporation's Electric Power Station on Newport Road, Roath, began supplying electricity in 1902 when the first electric trams ran in the city from the tram depot adjacent to the south of it. The power station was served by a siding off the Roath Branch of the Taff Vale Railway. Wooden cooling towers were superseded by two concrete ones, begun in 1941, completed by the middle of 1942 and subsequently camouflaged. The power station, including the cooling towers and the tram depot, were demolished in 1972.

Seven days before this photograph was taken, Mutiny on the Bounty *with Marlon Brando and Trevor Howard was released.*

Above: **CARDIFF** Working route 9 on 15 November is No 247 (EBO 904), an East Lancashire-bodied BUT 9641T new in 1950; it would be scrapped in 1966.

Frank Ifield with Lovesick Blues *was the No 1 single on this day.*

CARDIFF trolleybuses Nos 248 and 251 to 274 had bodywork completed by the local firm of Bruce, on East Lancashire frames. Representing the Bruce completed bodywork and nearing Pengam terminus, also on 15 November, is No 258 (EBO 915), a BUT 9641T new in 1950.

EASTBOURNE
Passing Eastbourne railway station on 30 June is No 20 (JK 9648), a Weymann-bodied AEC Regent III new in May 1947 and sold for scrap in June 1966. During 1960 this bus had received seats in the lower saloon from former London Transport trolleybuses.

COSHAM Turning out of Spur Road, Cosham, and heading south along Northern Road on 17 October is Portsmouth No 246 (RV 8328), an AEC 661T new in 1936 with bodywork by Cravens; it was later rebuilt by Portsmouth Corporation using Metal Sections fabrications.

The British International Motor Show opened at Earl's Court in London on this day and the Triumph Spitfire was among the new cars showcased during the event.

Right: **COSHAM** No 305 (ERV 930) turns left from Northern Road into the private road leading to Cosham Red Lion terminus. The 15 Burlingham bodied BUTs were used regularly from Cosham to North End, which gave a 5-minute service from Cosham to Copnor and Milton before the routes divided via Eastney (5/6) or Winter Road (A/B). No 303 was the unlucky one of the batch, being involved in an accident on 11 April 1961, and not considered worth repairing as the trolleybus replacement scheme was already well in hand. The rest of the batch remained in service until the end of the system on 27 July 1963.

Above: **PORTSMOUTH** Another of the rebuilds was No 273 (RV 9124), new in 1936. This view was taken on 17 October as 273 climbed Fratton Bridge on its way to Clarence Pier.

During that month the Guildhall presented a British package starring Billy Fury plus Marty Wilde, Mike Sarne, Jimmy Justice, Mark Wynter, Joe Brown, Karl Denver and Peter Jay & the Jaywalkers. On Friday 5 October Acker Bilk was at the Savoy.

Right: **PORTSMOUTH** Travelling southbound along Copnor Road near its junction with Madeira Road is No 259 (RV 9110), an AEC 661T new in 1936 with Cravens bodywork; this trolleybus also was rebuilt by Portsmouth Corporation using Metal Sections fabrications.

The No 1 album at this time was The Best of Ball, Barber and Bilk, *featuring Messrs Kenny, Chris and Acker.*

Right: **PORTSMOUTH** Also seen on Copnor Road on service G to Eastern Avenue is No 29 (EBK 566), an all-Crossley DD42/7T new in 1949. By 1965 the HOE engines and turbo converters of the remaining Crossleys had been replaced by diesel engines and gearboxes from scrapped Leyland TD4s. No 29 received the engine change, and remained in the fleet until 1967.

PORTSMOUTH Opposite the Milton White House trolleybus turning circle on the same day is No 188 (DTP 822), a Weymann-bodied Leyland PD1A, one of a batch of 19 PD1 and PD1As new in 1948; this example was withdrawn in 1967 after 18 years in service. Note that the Portsmouth City Coat of Arms' motto was in English, not Latin: 'Heaven's Light our Guide'.

Index of operators and their vehicles